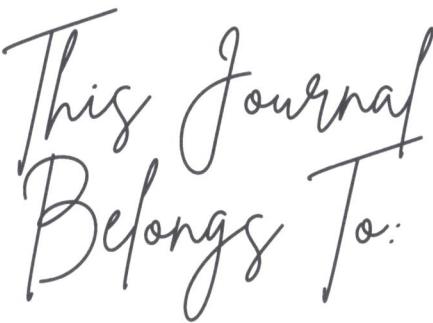

This Journal Belongs To:

_____

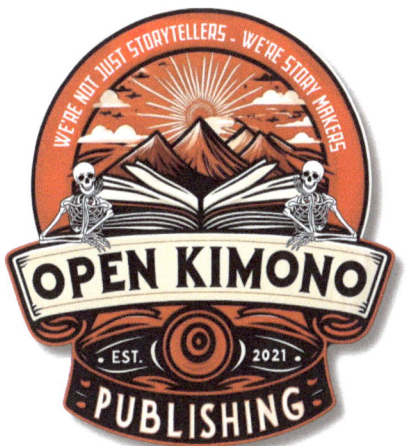

Copyright 2024 © Open Kimono Publishing, LLC
ISBN: 978-1-961763-15-9
All rights reserved.
No part of this journal may be reproduced, distributed, or transmitted in any form without the prior written permission of the publisher.

www.openkimonopublishing.com
www.x.com/openkimonopub

This Year is Going to be Your Year!

weekly planner

WEEK OF _____

MONDAY

TUESDAY

WEDNESDAY

THURSDAY

FRIDAY

SATURDAY

SUNDAY

PRIORITIES

TO-DO

_____
_____
_____
_____
_____
_____
_____
_____
_____
_____

NOTES

SUCCESSES THIS WEEK

_____
_____
_____
_____
_____

WEEKLY GRATITUDE

_____
_____
_____
_____
_____

AREAS FOR IMPROVMENT

_____
_____
_____
_____

weekly planner

WEEK OF _____

PRIORITIES

TO-DO

_____
_____
_____
_____
_____
_____
_____
_____
_____

NOTES

SUCCESSES THIS WEEK

_____
_____
_____
_____
_____

WEEKLY GRATITUDE

_____
_____
_____
_____
_____

AREAS FOR IMPROVMENT

_____
_____
_____
_____

weekly planner

WEEK OF _____

PRIORITIES

MONDAY

TUESDAY

WEDNESDAY

TO-DO

_____
_____
_____
_____
_____
_____
_____
_____
_____
_____

THURSDAY

FRIDAY

NOTES

SATURDAY

SUNDAY

SUCCESSES THIS WEEK

_____
_____
_____
_____
_____

WEEKLY GRATITUDE

_____
_____
_____
_____
_____

AREAS FOR IMPROVMENT

_____
_____
_____
_____

weekly planner

WEEK OF _____

MONDAY	
TUESDAY	
WEDNESDAY	
THURSDAY	
FRIDAY	
SATURDAY	
SUNDAY	

PRIORITIES

TO-DO

_____
_____
_____
_____
_____
_____
_____
_____
_____

NOTES

SUCCESSES THIS WEEK

WEEKLY GRATITUDE

AREAS FOR IMPROVMENT

---

weekly planner

WEEK OF_____

PRIORITIES

TO-DO

NOTES

SUCCESSES THIS WEEK

WEEKLY GRATITUDE

AREAS FOR IMPROVMENT

---

weekly planner

WEEK OF _____

MONDAY

TUESDAY

WEDNESDAY

THURSDAY

FRIDAY

SATURDAY

SUNDAY

PRIORITIES

TO-DO

_____
_____
_____
_____
_____
_____
_____
_____
_____
_____

NOTES

SUCCESSES THIS WEEK

_____
_____
_____
_____
_____

WEEKLY GRATITUDE

_____
_____
_____
_____
_____

AREAS FOR IMPROVMENT

_____
_____
_____
_____

weekly planner

WEEK OF _____

MONDAY	
TUESDAY	
WEDNESDAY	
THURSDAY	
FRIDAY	
SATURDAY	
SUNDAY	

PRIORITIES

TO-DO

_____
_____
_____
_____
_____
_____
_____
_____
_____
_____

NOTES

SUCCESSES THIS WEEK

WEEKLY GRATITUDE

AREAS FOR IMPROVMENT

---

weekly planner

MONDAY

TUESDAY

WEDNESDAY

THURSDAY

FRIDAY

SATURDAY

SUNDAY

WEEK OF _____

PRIORITIES

TO-DO

NOTES

SUCCESSES THIS WEEK

_____
_____
_____
_____
_____

WEEKLY GRATITUDE

_____
_____
_____
_____
_____

AREAS FOR IMPROVMENT

_____
_____
_____
_____

weekly planner

WEEK OF _____

| MONDAY |
| TUESDAY |
| WEDNESDAY |
| THURSDAY |
| FRIDAY |
| SATURDAY |
| SUNDAY |

PRIORITIES

TO-DO

_____
_____
_____
_____
_____
_____
_____
_____
_____

NOTES

SUCCESSES THIS WEEK

___
___
___
___
___
___

WEEKLY GRATITUDE

___
___
___
___
___

AREAS FOR IMPROVMENT

___
___
___
___

weekly planner

WEEK OF_____

MONDAY

TUESDAY

WEDNESDAY

THURSDAY

FRIDAY

SATURDAY

SUNDAY

PRIORITIES

TO-DO

_____
_____
_____
_____
_____
_____
_____
_____
_____
_____

NOTES

SUCCESSES THIS WEEK

WEEKLY GRATITUDE

AREAS FOR IMPROVMENT

---

weekly planner

WEEK OF _____

MONDAY

TUESDAY

WEDNESDAY

THURSDAY

FRIDAY

SATURDAY

SUNDAY

PRIORITIES

TO-DO

_____
_____
_____
_____
_____
_____
_____
_____
_____

NOTES

SUCCESSES THIS WEEK

_____
_____
_____
_____
_____
_____

WEEKLY GRATITUDE

_____
_____
_____
_____
_____
_____

AREAS FOR IMPROVMENT

_____
_____
_____
_____

weekly planner

WEEK OF _____

MONDAY	
TUESDAY	
WEDNESDAY	
THURSDAY	
FRIDAY	
SATURDAY	
SUNDAY	

PRIORITIES

TO-DO

_____
_____
_____
_____
_____
_____
_____
_____
_____
_____

NOTES

SUCCESSES THIS WEEK

_____
_____
_____
_____
_____

WEEKLY GRATITUDE

_____
_____
_____
_____
_____

AREAS FOR IMPROVMENT

_____
_____
_____
_____

weekly planner

WEEK OF _____

MONDAY

TUESDAY

WEDNESDAY

THURSDAY

FRIDAY

SATURDAY

SUNDAY

PRIORITIES

TO-DO

_____
_____
_____
_____
_____
_____
_____
_____
_____

NOTES

SUCCESSES THIS WEEK

_____
_____
_____
_____
_____

WEEKLY GRATITUDE

_____
_____
_____
_____
_____

AREAS FOR IMPROVMENT

_____
_____
_____
_____

weekly planner

WEEK OF _____

| MONDAY |
| TUESDAY |
| WEDNESDAY |
| THURSDAY |
| FRIDAY |
| SATURDAY |
| SUNDAY |

PRIORITIES

TO-DO

_____
_____
_____
_____
_____
_____
_____
_____
_____
_____

NOTES

SUCCESSES THIS WEEK

_____
_____
_____
_____
_____

WEEKLY GRATITUDE

_____
_____
_____
_____
_____

AREAS FOR IMPROVMENT

_____
_____
_____
_____

weekly planner

WEEK OF _____

MONDAY
TUESDAY
WEDNESDAY
THURSDAY
FRIDAY
SATURDAY
SUNDAY

PRIORITIES

TO-DO

_____
_____
_____
_____
_____
_____
_____
_____
_____
_____

NOTES

SUCCESSES THIS WEEK

WEEKLY GRATITUDE

AREAS FOR IMPROVMENT

---

weekly planner

WEEK OF _____

MONDAY

TUESDAY

WEDNESDAY

THURSDAY

FRIDAY

SATURDAY

SUNDAY

PRIORITIES

TO-DO

_____
_____
_____
_____
_____
_____
_____
_____
_____

NOTES

SUCCESSES THIS WEEK

WEEKLY GRATITUDE

AREAS FOR IMPROVMENT

---

weekly planner

WEEK OF _____

MONDAY

TUESDAY

WEDNESDAY

THURSDAY

FRIDAY

SATURDAY

SUNDAY

PRIORITIES

TO-DO

NOTES

SUCCESSES THIS WEEK

_____

_____

_____

_____

_____

WEEKLY GRATITUDE

_____

_____

_____

_____

_____

AREAS FOR IMPROVMENT

_____

_____

_____

_____

weekly planner

WEEK OF _____

MONDAY	
TUESDAY	
WEDNESDAY	
THURSDAY	
FRIDAY	
SATURDAY	
SUNDAY	

PRIORITIES

TO-DO

_____
_____
_____
_____
_____
_____
_____
_____
_____
_____

NOTES

SUCCESSES THIS WEEK

WEEKLY GRATITUDE

AREAS FOR IMPROVMENT

---

weekly planner

WEEK OF _____

MONDAY

TUESDAY

WEDNESDAY

THURSDAY

FRIDAY

SATURDAY

SUNDAY

PRIORITIES

TO-DO

_____
_____
_____
_____
_____
_____
_____
_____
_____

NOTES

SUCCESSES THIS WEEK

WEEKLY GRATITUDE

AREAS FOR IMPROVMENT

---

weekly planner

WEEK OF _____

| MONDAY |
| TUESDAY |
| WEDNESDAY |
| THURSDAY |
| FRIDAY |
| SATURDAY |
| SUNDAY |

PRIORITIES

TO-DO

_____
_____
_____
_____
_____
_____
_____
_____
_____
_____

NOTES

SUCCESSES THIS WEEK

_____
_____
_____
_____
_____
_____

WEEKLY GRATITUDE

_____
_____
_____
_____
_____

AREAS FOR IMPROVMENT

_____
_____
_____
_____

weekly planner

WEEK OF _____

MONDAY	

PRIORITIES

TUESDAY	

WEDNESDAY	

TO-DO

_____
_____
_____
_____
_____
_____
_____
_____
_____
_____

THURSDAY	

FRIDAY	

NOTES

SATURDAY	

SUNDAY	

SUCCESSES THIS WEEK

WEEKLY GRATITUDE

AREAS FOR IMPROVMENT

---

weekly planner

WEEK OF _____

MONDAY

TUESDAY

WEDNESDAY

THURSDAY

FRIDAY

SATURDAY

SUNDAY

PRIORITIES

TO-DO

_____
_____
_____
_____
_____
_____
_____
_____
_____

NOTES

SUCCESSES THIS WEEK

___

WEEKLY GRATITUDE

___

AREAS FOR IMPROVMENT

___

weekly planner

WEEK OF _____

MONDAY

TUESDAY

WEDNESDAY

THURSDAY

FRIDAY

SATURDAY

SUNDAY

PRIORITIES

TO-DO

_____
_____
_____
_____
_____
_____
_____
_____

NOTES

SUCCESSES THIS WEEK

WEEKLY GRATITUDE

AREAS FOR IMPROVMENT

---

weekly planner

WEEK OF _____

MONDAY

TUESDAY

WEDNESDAY

THURSDAY

FRIDAY

SATURDAY

SUNDAY

PRIORITIES

TO-DO

_____
_____
_____
_____
_____
_____
_____
_____
_____
_____

NOTES

SUCCESSES THIS WEEK

_____
_____
_____
_____
_____

WEEKLY GRATITUDE

_____
_____
_____
_____
_____

AREAS FOR IMPROVMENT

_____
_____
_____
_____

weekly planner

WEEK OF _____

MONDAY

TUESDAY

WEDNESDAY

THURSDAY

FRIDAY

SATURDAY

SUNDAY

PRIORITIES

TO-DO

_____
_____
_____
_____
_____
_____
_____
_____
_____

NOTES

SUCCESSES THIS WEEK

WEEKLY GRATITUDE

AREAS FOR IMPROVMENT

---

weekly planner

WEEK OF _____

MONDAY

TUESDAY

WEDNESDAY

THURSDAY

FRIDAY

SATURDAY

SUNDAY

PRIORITIES

TO-DO

_____
_____
_____
_____
_____
_____
_____
_____
_____

NOTES

SUCCESSES THIS WEEK

_____
_____
_____
_____
_____

WEEKLY GRATITUDE

_____
_____
_____
_____
_____

AREAS FOR IMPROVMENT

_____
_____
_____
_____

weekly planner

WEEK OF _____

MONDAY	
TUESDAY	
WEDNESDAY	
THURSDAY	
FRIDAY	
SATURDAY	
SUNDAY	

PRIORITIES

TO-DO

_____
_____
_____
_____
_____
_____
_____
_____
_____

NOTES

SUCCESSES THIS WEEK

_____
_____
_____
_____
_____
_____

WEEKLY GRATITUDE

_____
_____
_____
_____
_____
_____

AREAS FOR IMPROVMENT

_____
_____
_____
_____
_____

weekly planner

WEEK OF _____

MONDAY	

PRIORITIES

TUESDAY	

WEDNESDAY	

TO-DO

_____
_____
_____
_____

THURSDAY	

_____
_____
_____

FRIDAY	

_____
_____
_____

NOTES

SATURDAY	

SUNDAY	

SUCCESSES THIS WEEK

_____
_____
_____
_____
_____

WEEKLY GRATITUDE

_____
_____
_____
_____
_____

AREAS FOR IMPROVMENT

_____
_____
_____
_____

weekly planner

WEEK OF _____

MONDAY

TUESDAY

WEDNESDAY

THURSDAY

FRIDAY

SATURDAY

SUNDAY

PRIORITIES

TO-DO

_____
_____
_____
_____
_____
_____
_____
_____
_____
_____

NOTES

SUCCESSES THIS WEEK

_____
_____
_____
_____
_____

WEEKLY GRATITUDE

_____
_____
_____
_____
_____

AREAS FOR IMPROVMENT

_____
_____
_____
_____

weekly planner

WEEK OF _____

MONDAY	
TUESDAY	
WEDNESDAY	
THURSDAY	
FRIDAY	
SATURDAY	
SUNDAY	

PRIORITIES

TO-DO

_____
_____
_____
_____
_____
_____
_____
_____
_____
_____

NOTES

SUCCESSES THIS WEEK

WEEKLY GRATITUDE

AREAS FOR IMPROVMENT

---

weekly planner

WEEK OF _____

MONDAY

TUESDAY

WEDNESDAY

THURSDAY

FRIDAY

SATURDAY

SUNDAY

PRIORITIES

TO-DO

NOTES

SUCCESSES THIS WEEK

_____
_____
_____
_____
_____

WEEKLY GRATITUDE

_____
_____
_____
_____
_____

AREAS FOR IMPROVMENT

_____
_____
_____
_____

weekly planner

WEEK OF _____

| MONDAY |
| TUESDAY |
| WEDNESDAY |
| THURSDAY |
| FRIDAY |
| SATURDAY |
| SUNDAY |

PRIORITIES

TO-DO

_____
_____
_____
_____
_____
_____
_____
_____
_____
_____

NOTES

SUCCESSES THIS WEEK

_____
_____
_____
_____
_____

WEEKLY GRATITUDE

_____
_____
_____
_____
_____

AREAS FOR IMPROVMENT

_____
_____
_____
_____

weekly planner

WEEK OF _____

MONDAY	
TUESDAY	
WEDNESDAY	
THURSDAY	
FRIDAY	
SATURDAY	
SUNDAY	

PRIORITIES

TO-DO

_____
_____
_____
_____
_____
_____
_____
_____
_____
_____

NOTES

SUCCESSES THIS WEEK

_____
_____
_____
_____
_____

WEEKLY GRATITUDE

_____
_____
_____
_____
_____

AREAS FOR IMPROVMENT

_____
_____
_____
_____

weekly planner

MONDAY

TUESDAY

WEDNESDAY

THURSDAY

FRIDAY

SATURDAY

SUNDAY

WEEK OF _____

PRIORITIES

TO-DO

_____
_____
_____
_____
_____
_____
_____
_____
_____

NOTES

SUCCESSES THIS WEEK

_____

_____

_____

_____

_____

WEEKLY GRATITUDE

_____

_____

_____

_____

_____

AREAS FOR IMPROVMENT

_____

_____

_____

_____

weekly planner

WEEK OF _____

| MONDAY |
| TUESDAY |
| WEDNESDAY |
| THURSDAY |
| FRIDAY |
| SATURDAY |
| SUNDAY |

PRIORITIES

TO-DO

_____
_____
_____
_____
_____
_____
_____
_____
_____
_____

NOTES

SUCCESSES THIS WEEK

WEEKLY GRATITUDE

AREAS FOR IMPROVMENT

---

weekly planner

WEEK OF _____

MONDAY

TUESDAY

WEDNESDAY

THURSDAY

FRIDAY

SATURDAY

SUNDAY

PRIORITIES

TO-DO

NOTES

SUCCESSES THIS WEEK

WEEKLY GRATITUDE

AREAS FOR IMPROVMENT

---

weekly planner

WEEK OF_____

MONDAY
TUESDAY
WEDNESDAY
THURSDAY
FRIDAY
SATURDAY
SUNDAY

PRIORITIES

TO-DO

_____
_____
_____
_____
_____
_____
_____
_____
_____

NOTES

SUCCESSES THIS WEEK

_____
_____
_____
_____
_____
_____

WEEKLY GRATITUDE

_____
_____
_____
_____
_____
_____

AREAS FOR IMPROVMENT

_____
_____
_____
_____

weekly planner

WEEK OF _____

MONDAY

TUESDAY

WEDNESDAY

THURSDAY

FRIDAY

SATURDAY

SUNDAY

PRIORITIES

TO-DO

_____
_____
_____
_____
_____
_____
_____
_____
_____
_____

NOTES

SUCCESSES THIS WEEK

_____
_____
_____
_____
_____

WEEKLY GRATITUDE

_____
_____
_____
_____
_____

AREAS FOR IMPROVMENT

_____
_____
_____
_____

weekly planner

WEEK OF _____

MONDAY

TUESDAY

WEDNESDAY

THURSDAY

FRIDAY

SATURDAY

SUNDAY

PRIORITIES

TO-DO

_____
_____
_____
_____
_____
_____
_____
_____
_____

NOTES

SUCCESSES THIS WEEK

_____
_____
_____
_____
_____
_____

WEEKLY GRATITUDE

_____
_____
_____
_____
_____
_____

AREAS FOR IMPROVMENT

_____
_____
_____
_____
_____

weekly planner

WEEK OF _____

MONDAY

TUESDAY

WEDNESDAY

THURSDAY

FRIDAY

SATURDAY

SUNDAY

PRIORITIES

TO-DO

_____
_____
_____
_____
_____
_____
_____
_____
_____
_____

NOTES

SUCCESSES THIS WEEK

_____
_____
_____
_____
_____

WEEKLY GRATITUDE

_____
_____
_____
_____
_____

AREAS FOR IMPROVMENT

_____
_____
_____
_____

weekly planner

MONDAY

TUESDAY

WEDNESDAY

THURSDAY

FRIDAY

SATURDAY

SUNDAY

WEEK OF _____

PRIORITIES

TO-DO

_____
_____
_____
_____
_____
_____
_____
_____
_____

NOTES

SUCCESSES THIS WEEK

WEEKLY GRATITUDE

AREAS FOR IMPROVMENT

---

weekly planner

WEEK OF _____

| MONDAY |
| TUESDAY |
| WEDNESDAY |
| THURSDAY |
| FRIDAY |
| SATURDAY |
| SUNDAY |

PRIORITIES

TO-DO

_____
_____
_____
_____
_____
_____
_____
_____
_____

NOTES

SUCCESSES THIS WEEK

WEEKLY GRATITUDE

AREAS FOR IMPROVMENT

---

weekly planner

WEEK OF _____

MONDAY	
TUESDAY	
WEDNESDAY	
THURSDAY	
FRIDAY	
SATURDAY	
SUNDAY	

PRIORITIES

TO-DO

_____
_____
_____
_____
_____
_____
_____
_____
_____

NOTES

SUCCESSES THIS WEEK

_____
_____
_____
_____
_____

WEEKLY GRATITUDE

_____
_____
_____
_____
_____

AREAS FOR IMPROVMENT

_____
_____
_____
_____

weekly planner

WEEK OF _____

| MONDAY |
| TUESDAY |
| WEDNESDAY |
| THURSDAY |
| FRIDAY |
| SATURDAY |
| SUNDAY |

PRIORITIES

TO-DO

_____
_____
_____
_____
_____
_____
_____
_____
_____
_____

NOTES

SUCCESSES THIS WEEK

_____
_____
_____
_____
_____

WEEKLY GRATITUDE

_____
_____
_____
_____
_____

AREAS FOR IMPROVMENT

_____
_____
_____
_____

weekly planner

WEEK OF _____

MONDAY	
TUESDAY	
WEDNESDAY	
THURSDAY	
FRIDAY	
SATURDAY	
SUNDAY	

PRIORITIES

TO-DO

_____
_____
_____
_____
_____
_____
_____
_____
_____
_____

NOTES

SUCCESSES THIS WEEK

WEEKLY GRATITUDE

AREAS FOR IMPROVMENT

---

weekly planner

WEEK OF _____

MONDAY

TUESDAY

WEDNESDAY

THURSDAY

FRIDAY

SATURDAY

SUNDAY

PRIORITIES

TO-DO

NOTES

SUCCESSES THIS WEEK

WEEKLY GRATITUDE

AREAS FOR IMPROVMENT

---

weekly planner

WEEK OF _____

| MONDAY |
| TUESDAY |
| WEDNESDAY |
| THURSDAY |
| FRIDAY |
| SATURDAY |
| SUNDAY |

PRIORITIES

TO-DO

_____
_____
_____
_____
_____
_____
_____
_____
_____
_____

NOTES

SUCCESSES THIS WEEK

_____
_____
_____
_____
_____

WEEKLY GRATITUDE

_____
_____
_____
_____
_____

AREAS FOR IMPROVMENT

_____
_____
_____
_____

weekly planner

WEEK OF _____

MONDAY	
TUESDAY	
WEDNESDAY	
THURSDAY	
FRIDAY	
SATURDAY	
SUNDAY	

PRIORITIES

TO-DO

_____
_____
_____
_____
_____
_____
_____
_____
_____
_____

NOTES

SUCCESSES THIS WEEK

_____
_____
_____
_____
_____

WEEKLY GRATITUDE

_____
_____
_____
_____
_____

AREAS FOR IMPROVMENT

_____
_____
_____
_____

weekly planner

WEEK OF _____

MONDAY	
TUESDAY	
WEDNESDAY	
THURSDAY	
FRIDAY	
SATURDAY	
SUNDAY	

PRIORITIES

TO-DO

_____
_____
_____
_____
_____
_____
_____
_____
_____

NOTES

SUCCESSES THIS WEEK

WEEKLY GRATITUDE

AREAS FOR IMPROVMENT

---

weekly planner

WEEK OF _____

PRIORITIES

TO-DO

NOTES

MONDAY

TUESDAY

WEDNESDAY

THURSDAY

FRIDAY

SATURDAY

SUNDAY

SUCCESSES THIS WEEK

_____
_____
_____
_____
_____

WEEKLY GRATITUDE

_____
_____
_____
_____
_____

AREAS FOR IMPROVMENT

_____
_____
_____
_____

weekly planner

WEEK OF _____

MONDAY

TUESDAY

WEDNESDAY

THURSDAY

FRIDAY

SATURDAY

SUNDAY

PRIORITIES

TO-DO

_____
_____
_____
_____
_____
_____
_____
_____
_____

NOTES

SUCCESSES THIS WEEK

_____
_____
_____
_____
_____

WEEKLY GRATITUDE

_____
_____
_____
_____
_____

AREAS FOR IMPROVMENT

_____
_____
_____
_____

weekly planner

WEEK OF _____

MONDAY	
TUESDAY	
WEDNESDAY	
THURSDAY	
FRIDAY	
SATURDAY	
SUNDAY	

PRIORITIES

TO-DO

_____
_____
_____
_____
_____
_____
_____
_____
_____

NOTES

SUCCESSES THIS WEEK

_____
_____
_____
_____
_____

WEEKLY GRATITUDE

_____
_____
_____
_____
_____

AREAS FOR IMPROVMENT

_____
_____
_____
_____

Notes

Notes

Notes

Notes

Notes

Notes

Notes

Notes

Notes

Notes

Notes

Notes

Notes

Notes

Notes

Notes

Notes

www.ingramcontent.com/pod-product-compliance
Lightning Source LLC
Chambersburg PA
CBHW041452010526
44107CB00013B/1016